MYSTERIES UNWRAPPED:
LOST CIVILIZATIONS

WRITTEN BY
SHARON LINNÉA

ILLUSTRATED BY
JOSH COCHRAN

STERLING

New York / London
www.sterlingpublishing.com/kids

STERLING and the distinctive Sterling logo are registered trademarks of
Sterling Publishing Co., Inc.

Library of Congress Cataloging-in-Publication Data

Linnéa, Sharon, 1956-
  Mysteries unwrapped. Lost civilizations / written by Sharon Linnéa ; illustrated by Josh Cochran.
    p. cm.
  Includes bibliographical references and index.
  ISBN 978-1-4027-3984-2
  1. Civilization, Ancient--Juvenile literature. 2. Extinct cities--Juvenile literature. 3. Lost continents--
Juvenile literature. 4. Archaeology--Juvenile literature. 5. Ur (Extinct city)--Juvenile literature.
6. Mayas--Juvenile literature. 7. Atlantis (Legendary place)--Juvenile literature. 8. Pompeii (Extinct
city)--Juvenile literature. 9. Angkor Wat (Angkor)--Juvenile literature. I. Cochran, Josh. II. Title. III.
Title: Lost civilizations.
  CB311.L56 2009
  930--dc22

                                                                                          2008042789

10 9 8 7 6 5 4 3 2 1

Published by Sterling Publishing Co., Inc.
387 Park Avenue South, New York, NY 10016
Text © 2009 by Sharon Linnéa
Illustrations © 2009 by Josh Cochran
Distributed in Canada by Sterling Publishing
c/o Canadian Manda Group, 165 Dufferin Street
Toronto, Ontario, Canada M6K 3H6
Distributed in the United Kingdom by GMC Distribution Services
Castle Place, 166 High Street, Lewes, East Sussex, England BN7 1XU
Distributed in Australia by Capricorn Link (Australia) Pty. Ltd.
P.O. Box 704, Windsor, NSW 2756, Australia

Printed in China
All rights reserved

Sterling ISBN 978-1-4027-3984-2

Book design by Joshua Moore of beardandglasses.com

For information about custom editions, special sales, premium and
corporate purchases, please contact Sterling Special Sales
Department at 800-805-5489 or specialsales@sterlingpublishing.com.

"ONE MUST ASK, WHAT HAS BECOME OF THIS POWERFUL RACE, SO CIVILIZED AND ENLIGHTENED TO CREATE THESE GIGANTIC WORKS? OH, SAD FRAGILITY OF HUMAN BEINGS!"
—HENRI MAHOUT

CONTENTS

INTRODUCTION

In the Fertile Crescent—the area of land in the Middle East where we believe the first humans walked—a giant walled city called Ur rose from the newly tamed Earth. For hundreds of years, farmers, craftsmen, musicians, scribes, lawyers, kings, and priests lived here, building enormous temples, writing plays, and crafting fine jewelry. Ur is even mentioned in the Bible. But for nearly 2,000 years, this once-proud city was lost, buried under tons of blowing sand. Could anyone bring it back to life?

Meanwhile, half a world away in the jungles of Central America, the Mayan culture thrived. The Mayan people built cities with large palaces, temples, pyramids, plazas, and boulevards. Then, after nearly 2,000 years, the cities were abandoned and millions of people vanished. Simply vanished. The lush, tropical plant life quickly overtook their structures and concealed the evidence of their civilization, as though it had never existed. For centuries, no one suspected the story of an entire people was buried here. Where did they go?

The philosopher Plato told many stories to help his followers think about how to live good lives. One of his favorite tales included a fabulous country called Atlantis. It had fertile farmland, gleaming houses, great universities, and awe-inspiring houses of worship. The story claims that this society met its destruction and sank into the ocean in the space of only a single night and day. What made this tale fascinating to Plato's listeners was that Plato insisted the story was true. Ever since, people have been in search of Atlantis. Where could it be?

In 79 A.D., Pompeii was a thriving city of 20,000 people. Pompeii had schools, a two-story shopping mall, theaters, gyms, and great restaurants—some with salad bars. But at noon on August 24, catastrophe struck. The giant volcano behind Pompeii exploded. Within twenty-four hours, everyone who had stayed in the city was dead—preserved exactly as they had been in their final moments. Pompeii was an eerie snapshot of a people, frozen in time, under tons of volcanic pumice and ash. Would the light of day ever shine on Pompeii again?

In the middle of the Cambodian jungle, a fantastic temple stood. It was larger than the great cathedrals of Europe, or any of the pyramids. It was surrounded by a city that held over 1,000 temples! The people who lived there thought their empire would last forever...until it was abandoned and became the stuff of legend. Who had lived there? Who would find their incredible work?

Join adventurous archeologists as they battle snakes, sandstorms, scorpions, and centuries of debris to unearth hidden civilizations lost to us—until now.

1. UR REDISCOVERED

In the early afternoon of June 19, 1617, an Italian nobleman named Pietro della Valle stood in the midst of a dry, barren plain. He was in southern Mesopotamia, in what is present-day Iraq. With him stood his wife, a beautiful young Syrian princess named Maani, and the local guides who had brought them there. As far as anyone knew, no European had ever before stood where they stood or saw what they saw.

They were looking at a mound of dirt. It wasn't just any mound of dirt, it was gigantic. It measured nearly two miles long, and it towered almost seventy feet up against the sky. Almost as puzzling was a line of smaller mounds heading off to the northeast. Mysterious, too, were the hundreds of ancient bricks littering the ground. The bricks were made from mud, bound together with pitch, and stamped in the middle with a strange form of writing.

The ruins had an ancient, exotic feeling. What were they? Pietro had no idea that he was gazing at ruins that would become known as one of the most important archeological finds in history.

Pietro and Maani traveled on and visited other locations in Asia. They brought home to Europe some important discoveries, including coffee, terrycloth towels, and even Persian cats.

But the citizens of the flood plain in southern Mesopotamia, dead and buried with their astonishing culture, continued to keep their secrets for another 300 years.

FIRST THINGS FIRST

For centuries, people living in a region of the Middle East formerly known as Mesopotamia knew of the ruins. It was hard to miss a mound of dirt that large. After Pietro's descriptions, Europeans knew about the ruins, too. But the territory was not easy for outsiders to reach—which, in many ways, was a good thing.

The science of archeology—discovering and studying ancient places and things—has only existed for about 150 years. Up to that time, most people who made their living finding ancient sites were called treasure hunters. They were looking for valuable jewels, gold, art, and antiquities that they could sell for a lot of money. Many sites the world over were plundered and their treasures sold to the wealthy as souvenirs.

It wasn't until the 1700s, that people began to realize that the chain of events told by the past was important and could help us understand human culture. People became more careful and thoughtful about digging up ancient ruins. They did so in a way that made it possible to preserve and explore the stories of the people who lived there. They didn't just grab what could be sold.

Archeology was still a new science when a British diplomat named J. E. Taylor went back to Tell al-Muqayyar, the town where Pietro found the ruins, and began to excavate the site in 1853. He only spent two seasons there, but it was long enough to make two important discoveries.

First, he discovered that the huge structure was a grand ziggurat—a building that the ancient people believed connected the people of Earth to the gods in heaven. The Ziggurat of Ur was incredible—at one time it had seven levels stretching to the sky. At the very top was a temple. Pietro had been right in one regard—the ancient bricks were very well made, and much of the ziggurat structure remained intact under layers of mud and dirt.

As he worked, J. E. Taylor discovered four cylinders with the same strange writing that Pietro had puzzled over. By this time, the writing had been identified as cuneiform. Linguists had only recently discovered a set of writings that included the same text in three languages. One of these was cuneiform. Since linguists could read the other languages, they could now compare the cuneiform with the languages that they understood and begin to crack the code. Taylor sent the cylinders to Henry Rawlinson, who had been involved in deciphering this ancient language.

Rawlinson deciphered the writing on the columns and made a historic pronouncement: the city J. E. Taylor had found was nothing less than the ancient city of Ur—one of the first cities in human history!

A clay tablet displays cuneiform characters used for counting the number of sheep and goats, found in southern Mesopotamia near Ur. (©GIANNI DAGLI ORTI/CORBIS)

CUNEIFORM

Inventing a system of writing changed civilization forever. For the first time, people could keep records of business transactions, tell stories of their gods, have a written system of laws that didn't change from day to day, and begin to record history.

The kind of writing invented in Ur and the surrounding city-states was called "cuneiform" (*kune-ey-uh-form*). It began as simple tally marks to record farming transactions. Next, drawn pictures of animals or crops were added. The biggest jump came when people developed symbols for words instead of always drawing pictures. In other words, there was a symbol for "cow" that wasn't simply a picture of a cow. Once symbols became standard, cuneiform took off in a big way. People even wrote down jokes and riddles such as this one:

Riddle: A HOUSE THAT ONE ENTERS BLIND AND LEAVES SEEING...
Answer: A SCHOOL

The people of Ur also developed court systems, and a written code of law, called the "Code of Ur-Nammu." It is considered the oldest surviving written set of laws, created in approximately 2050 B.C. It listed court procedures, penalties for misdeeds, tax codes, and ceremonial laws. It paved the way for important collections of laws such as the Code of Hammurabi, the Ten Commandments and the laws of the Torah, and finally the Magna Carta. Each of these was an important step on the path to developing a civilization governed by law.

RAWLINSON DECIPHERED THE WRITING ON THE COLUMNS AND MADE A HISTORIC PRONOUNCEMENT: THE CITY J. E. TAYLOR HAD FOUND WAS NOTHING LESS THAN THE ANCIENT CITY OF UR—ONE OF THE FIRST CITIES IN HUMAN HISTORY!

Ur had been first a settlement, then an important city in Mesopotamia—the place where humans first formed civilization—and survived for nearly 5,000 years. (In contrast, the United States has existed as the United States for fewer than 250 years.) Ur was even mentioned in the Bible as the hometown of Abraham and his wife, Sarah—the founding father and mother of the Jewish people.

The worldwide excitement over this discovery was enormous. But was anything besides the ziggurat still there?

THE BIG DIG BEGINS

Even after the excitement of the discovery of Ur, it took a long time for someone to return there. Seventy years passed before a famous English archeologist named Leonard Woolley got the financing to come back to Tell al-Muqayyar. He wanted to do a proper dig and find out what was there.

Woolley and his team began by digging two large trenches parallel to the ziggurat—calling them Trench A and Trench B. Within the week, they uncovered an ancient wall and the evidence of several ancient buildings in Trench B.

As exciting as that was, it paled in comparison to what they found in Trench A. Within that same week, they knew Trench A was an incredibly important find. The first thing they discovered were human burials. In these graves they found not only skeletons but also incredible jewelry made of gemstones and precious metals such as carnelian, lapis lazuli, and gold.

Woolley could tell it was only a small taste of what was to come.

The whole camp was buzzing with excitement about what might be found in Trench A, which they nicknamed "the gold trench." Woolley called them all together and made an announcement: as a team, they were not yet experienced enough to dig out the burials. They had to earn the right by excavating other parts of the site so carefully that they would be ready to find out what was in the treasure trove of the gold trench.

Although everyone was disappointed, they got busy working on Trench B.

And the ancient city of Ur began to come to life once more.

THE ANCIENT WORLD ACCORDING TO LEONARD WOOLLEY

The people who worked with Woolley all agreed he had two great talents, both of which were necessary for the discoveries at Ur. One was that he was a trained and experienced archeologist, who knew how to unearth important objects very carefully, catalogue them, and understand what he found.

But his second talent was just as important. Those who knew Woolley, read his articles, or visited Ur all agreed: Woolley was a master storyteller. As he took people through the dig at Ur, he told fascinating stories of what had happened there thousands of years ago. Many people said hearing Woolley talk made you believe you were really experiencing the life of the ancient culture of Ur.

For example, Woolley didn't just say Ur was the home of Abraham and Sarah, he would take you over to one of the parts of the city whose ruins were from the time of Abraham, and show you around Abraham's own house! Of course, he couldn't prove for certain that that particular house really belonged to Abraham—but no one could prove it didn't!

Here are the facts from some of the stories he told.

THE GENERAL TAKES COMMAND

When ancient peoples stopped migrating and began settling in communities throughout the area known as Mesopotamia (which means "between the rivers" of the Tigris and Euphrates) a number of large cities were settled, including Ur. We call them "city-states" because each had its own government. The people of these cities spoke the same language and did business with each other. They also fought each other on a regular basis to decide which city, or which king, was supreme ruler.

Each of the city-states in the area had its fortunes rise and fall many times over the millennia, depending on who was in charge.

About 2,500 years after Ur was settled—and about 2,500 years before Jesus was born—it was conquered by a king named Ur-Nammu.

Ur-Nammu was a brilliant man and a keen strategist. When he got to Ur, he found a thriving city with fertile farmlands, and two ports for shipping and trading on the Euphrates River. Ur-Nammu decided to make Ur his capital city. Over the next decade, his kingdom grew as he conquered and united the territories now known as Iraq and western Iran.

Ur-Nammu and his son, Shulgi, ushered in the Golden Age of Ur. They chose the moon god Nanna as the principal god of Ur. They built the ziggurat with a temple on top to worship him, and surrounded it with a section of town where the priests and priestesses lived. The land was called Sumer, and the people were known as Sumerians. They believed that the high priests and the king not only led the worship of gods but also were gods themselves.

EVERYDAY LIFE IN UR

Even if you weren't a priest or a king, everyday life in Ur wasn't half bad. Farmers had advanced systems of irrigation, which brought water to their crops. The arts, such as music and story-telling thrived, and craftsmen were very highly trained. They made not only city streets out of brick but also very comfortable two-story houses, each with a private courtyard in back. Merchants sailed from the ports at Ur, trading food and crafts as far away as Turkey, bringing back precious gems and exotic spices and fabrics.

Middle-class houses had another unique feature: the family graveyard was in the basement. Under the houses, the archeologists discovered not only the remains of deceased family members but also often of their dogs—sure proof that in Ur, the pet was a "member of the family."

OPPOSITE PAGE: A boy heards goats in front of the Ziggurat of Ur in 1964. The remains of the city walls can be seen in the foreground. The city ruins and the death pits are behind the ziggurat. (©DAVID LEES/CORBIS)

SCHOOL DAYS

As the culture of Ur advanced, it became necessary to create schools to pass on the civilization's many inventions including writing, bookkeeping, and the court system. In Ur, only the sons of the wealthy went to school. The children of the lower classes, the slaves, and even the children of the farmers were expected to stay home and help with the family business.

It was a mixed blessing to be a schoolboy in Ur. The school day was twelve hours long or more, running from sun up to dark. The teacher was the master of the schoolroom. Lessons were painstakingly scratched into clay, and students were routinely beaten with a rod for giving a wrong answer, not working hard enough, being late, or having a bad attitude.

Archeologists found a 4,000-year-old diary entry from a student in Ur. In it he told how he begged his father to have his teacher over for dinner. When the teacher came, they fed him well, gave him good wine, and even a bribe. After that, to the boy's great relief, he received fewer beatings in the classroom!

THE BEST PART OF TOWN

The best houses in the best part of town belonged to the priests and priestesses of Nanna, the moon god. According to book-keeping tablets found in Ur, a huge portion of people's incomes in Ur went to finance the temple and the priests who ran it. However, since the people believed their rulers were divine, and their blessing was necessary to ensure the continued success of Ur and its citizens, they anted up both the money and man-power necessary to build a ziggurat and allowed the priests to live in luxury. The high priests and priestesses had the finest of everything: houses, food, servants, and jewelry. Stunning neck-laces, bracelets, rings, and earrings were found under the floor in the home of a high priestess.

The original Ziggurat of Ur-Nammu was five stories tall. Four thousand years ago, it must have seemed spectacular. The people of Ur believed the ziggurat was so tall that the gods from heaven could come down and commune with the people of Earth in the temple built on the very top. Because of this, only the highest priest or priestess was allowed to enter this top level. Other priests could enter the other parts of the ziggurat, but the common folk had to wait below for the priests to return and tell them what the gods had to say.

In Ur, the priests recorded and passed along stories about the gods. They also performed rituals to ensure good harvests and bountiful trading.

The kings, priests, and priestesses also had many servants, musicians, entertainers, jewelers, and guards at their beck and call. Being considered divine certainly had its advantages!

DYING FOR A GOOD JOB

The men and women excavating Ur were excited when, at the beginning of the fifth year, Woolley determined they were ready to start work on the "gold trench."

When they did, Woolley's fondest dreams came true. It was an incredible find! Altogether they found about 1,850 burials. While many of them seemed to be the remains of ordinary people, sixteen of them were buried in such a grand style that Woolley dubbed them the "Royal Tombs." No one was certain if the men and women buried in these graves were kings and queens, or priests and priestesses, or a combination of the two. What we do know is that they went in style!

The men and women buried in the Royal Tombs were found with riches like gold and silver, gemstones, tools, finely crafted weapons, exquisite jewelry, games, and musical instruments. For example, the tomb of King Meskalamdug contained a golden helmet that had been crafted to look exactly like the hair style of the time, as well as a sword with a golden handle and a sheath made of fine filigree.

More chilling, they discovered that, if you were in the court of the king or queen, your job didn't end when the ruler you served died. One king was found buried not only with riches but also with fifty-nine members of his court. Soldiers with their weapons, musicians with their instruments, and servants with food and drink all followed the body of the king into his tomb, were carefully arranged according to their rank and their job, and then drank poison, laid down, and died—to go and continue serving their king in the next life.

Woolley described what happened with the grave of a woman named Puabi, who was either a queen or the highest priestess. When she died, she was dressed in her most beautiful robes and finest jewelry. Then she was carried on a bier into the inner room of her tomb. Her two favorite servants went with her. Those two women drank poison and died. The door was shut, and the three were walled in to their tomb.

Then down into the empty pit in front of the tomb there came a procession of people, the members of Puabi's court, in all their finery. There were brightly colored garments; head-dresses of carnelian and lapis lazuli, silver and gold; officers with insignia of their rank; and even oxen pulling a cart. There were six male servants, four female harpists, and sixty-four ladies of the court. In all, seventy-four people died to accompany their ruler.

Woolley's dig ended after twelve seasons. (The "season" for archeologists to work in Iraq ran from autumn until early spring of the next year. During the summer it was too hot to continue to work. They had to go home to England and return again the next fall.) While Woolley's team dug many parts of Ur, many other parts remain untouched, waiting for the political situation in Iraq to stabilize, so that archeologists might begin to dig once more.

THE SUN SETS ON UR

After the reign of Ur-Nammu and his son Shulgi, the rulers of Ur were never as strong. Other civilizations eventually took over, including the Assyrians and the Babylonians. They used other cities, such as Babylon, as their capital instead of Ur. Over the period of less than 100 years, the course of the Euphrates River moved ten miles to the east, and Ur was no longer a port.

Toward the end of Ur's living history, one king "gave" the city to his daughter, the high priestess of Nanna. She is the one who added two more stories to the ziggurat. However grand the ziggurat was, the city never became an important trade center again. Depending on who was ruling this area of Mesopotamia, the religions changed, and the worship of Nanna became unimportant. The people eventually moved to more prosperous cities.

The sand took over. And the stunningly advanced culture that had thrived at the dawn of human civilization waited under the Earth to be discovered once more.

2.

THE MAYA

John Lloyd Stephens thought of himself as an explorer as much as a diplomat. As American ambassador to Central America in 1839, Stephens had witnessed a civil war and had sent back harrowing dispatches. But by November of that year, he was a man on a mission to discover the hidden history of British Honduras (now named Belize). At the time, the country was sparsely populated. Most of the native people lived in mud huts clustered in small villages.

Stephens was traveling with a fellow explorer, an English architect and artist named Frederick Catherwood. Both men had heard tall tales about kings and queens, human sacrifice, and fantastic cities that boasted buildings taller than those in New York at that time. Could there have been an ancient civilization there, as splendid as the stories told?

On November 17, 1839, Stephens and Catherwood took a trek into the jungle near the coast. The first thing the men noticed that seemed out of the ordinary was part of a stone wall that appeared to be man-made. Before long they saw it was not only huge, it was intricately carved. It didn't take long for them to realize they'd walked into the center of a huge, abandoned city! It was nearly completely intact under the overgrowth of the jungle. They were surrounded by temples, palaces, pyramids, and walkways.

"I am entering abruptly onto new ground!" Stephens wrote in excitement that night. He knew that in the space of that one day, the understanding of the history of Central America had changed for good.

That city—which today we know as Copán—stood on land that Stephens was able to buy for just $50. He and Catherwood spent two weeks uncovering as much as they could, and mapping it all out. Filled with excitement and high spirits, they took off on a dangerous journey into the jungle to see if they could find any other ancient sites.

By the time they returned to the United States the next June, they had found forty-four cities! It was clear a vast civilization had once covered the whole area. Within a century, archeologists would realize that at its zenith, a million people had lived in Belize alone!

In fact, the civilization of the Mayan people—which recent estimates say included 10 to 20 million people—extended over all of Central America and Mexico. It had more than 200 cities, twenty of which had more than 20,000 inhabitants, and half a dozen with a population of over 100,000! Not only that, the Maya had understood mathematics, astronomy, and architecture in very advanced ways. For thousands of years, the kings, queens, and priests who ruled lived a lavish lifestyle. Usually, the common people were well fed, healthy, and had a good standard of living. Then, almost overnight, the entire culture vanished. It simply vanished.

By the time the Spanish arrived in the mid-1500s, the Maya had become what could be considered a ghost of their former glorious civilization. The remaining Maya were easily conquered—and more than half of them were immediately killed by diseases (like the measles) that the Europeans had brought with them. To make matters worse, in 1561, a Spanish bishop named Diego de Landa made it his duty to burn all the Maya holy books and history books, called "codices." He felt they told stories of demons and superstitions. Consequently, 2,000 years of culture and history, painstakingly written down, literally went up in smoke. The remaining Mayan priests were beside themselves with grief—as were the archeologists who would later hear of this event.

From the time Stephens and Catherwood returned home to write of their exciting finds, hundreds of archeologists have descended upon the Central American jungles to uncover the fascinating story of the Maya. We now know much about how they lived and died and worshipped. But how and why they disappeared remains one of the great mysteries of all time.

HISTORY BOOKS OF STONE

Mayan priests wrote on bark from trees as well as on other materials such as stone, plaster and ceramics. They assembled these pages into books, sometimes covered in jaguar skins. Thirty large books were lost when Bishop Diego de Landa burned them. But, fortunately, the cities themselves were covered with picture writing called hieroglyphs which told the stories of each king and his glorious deeds. Hieroglyphs were found on wood, stone, plaster and ceramics. Archeologists studied these texts for decades. Finally, in the 1950s, they figured out the Maya had a picture "alphabet" of 350 glyphs or symbols, and they began to decipher what each one meant. In 1960, a Russian linguist was able to decipher the Mayan dates, and we could suddenly tell when—to the day—these great events occurred.

A ROYAL PAIN

Being a Mayan king or queen was a wonderful thing. (At times it could be painful.) Kings, queens, and priests were thought of as divine, and it was believed they could talk directly to the gods who could grant rain, children, success in battle, and plentiful crops. The Mayans lived in a harsh environment where hurricanes, drought, earthquakes, and warfare were common. This meant that communication with, and the pleasing of, the gods was so important that the common people felt it was in their own best interests to support the kings and priests in fine style.

To that end, they built palaces and temples in the shape of pyramids that seemed to touch the sky. Unlike Egyptian pyramids, these Mayan structures were built with a flat top, which housed a temple complex. They built huge plazas and walkways that were smoothed over and whitewashed so that they glistened brilliantly in the sun. The rulers got the best clothing and the best food. They had craftsmen and artists who gave them jewelry, masks, and clothing made with rare skins and feathers. They even went to war when the king told them it was time to do so.

In return, the royalty played their part. They dispensed divine knowledge, usually based on mathematics and astronomy—subjects that most common folk didn't know. They also gave their own blood (in very painful rituals) as a sacrifice for the gods.

A view of the Grand Plaza from the Central Acropolis in Tikal. This city was the largest one in the Mayan civilization and is located in Guatemala. These pyramids were once whitewashed and dazzling. When the priests and kings stood at the top, they were so high they appeared to be between heaven and earth.
(© ATLANTIDE PHOTOTRAVEL/CORBIS)

MAYAN MATHEMATICS

One reason the Maya had such a highly developed civilization was because, thousands of years ago, a Mayan mathematician came up with the concept of zero as a placeholder. The significance of this development is sometimes hard for us to understand. After all, we have been brought up with an understanding that "0" means nothing, and "20" means two sets of 10 with nothing left over. Throughout human history, however, there has been a huge rift between societies that invented zero and those that didn't. Simply put, if you have a zero, you can add, subtract, multiply, and divide numbers into infinity. If you don't, you can't.

The fact that the Maya had developed the concept of zero long before the birth of Jesus made possible great strides in every aspect of their life: architecture, economics, and, especially astronomy. (In contrast, they never invented the wheel, never figured out the use of metals—which would have helped a lot in a jungle environment!—and didn't realize they could use animals such as mules, horses, or even dogs, to help with transportation or labor.)

Unlike societies like those in Ur, or in ancient Greece and Rome, the Mayan priests had no intention of creating schools to educate the common people. They kept the understanding of math, science, religion, and architecture to themselves, and used their knowledge to prove they were divine.

When a baby was born to the king and queen and was chosen to be the new heir, a giant festival was given. Thousands of people would crowd the plaza below the huge royal mountain (which is what they called the pyramids). Important guests from other cities would come as well. The occasion was so important that it called for blood-letting. The king and queen would both pierce themselves and catch their blood on a sacred cloth, which would be burned, making the sacrifice complete. They believed that the gods would join them through these rituals, their spirits entering the world through wounds, and smile on the future of the infant.

Royalty even looked different from the commoners. Shortly after royal babies were born, boards were bound to the baby's skull in front and back, molding the soft parts of the skull so the head would be flat and tall. Being cross-eyed was considered a sign of wisdom and beauty, so when the child was a toddler, his or her mother would hang an ornament down between the youngster's eyes. But it was probably hard for the common folk to notice these things, because the king always appeared far above them on the royal mountain, and always wore a fearsome mask—sometimes covering his whole head and sometimes as large as his whole body.

The absolute power held by royalty and priests kept things organized. Crops were planted, reservoirs were built, and buildings were positioned in exactly the right places to follow the path of the sun, moon, and planet Venus.

MAYAN RELIGION (ALL ROADS LEAD TO DEATH)

The Maya believed that the gods were intimately involved in every facet of life. There were gods of the corn, of war, of fertility. Each day of the Mayan calendar was overseen by a particular god, so your birthday dictated which god would govern your life.

According to the Maya, the world was made up of three parts. The lower part, the Underworld, was called "Xibalba," and was inhabited by the gods of death and disease. The Middle World was where humans lived. The upper part, the Upper World, was a place of eternal peace and plenty. The Tree of Life grew through it all, having roots in the Underworld, the trunk in the Middle World, and its branches overarching the Upper World.

Most of the Mayans' attention was focused on appeasing the gods in this life, the Middle World, and on preparing for their harrowing and very dangerous journey through Xibalba. The gods who lived in the nine levels of Xibalba, also called "the frightful place," were evil and vengeful. All people had to journey through Xibalba after they died to make it to the Upper World. Many would not make it. They would remain in this terrible place of torture forever.

(Among the tortures there included demons with breath so terrible it could knock you out. They apparently also passed gas that was so toxic the Mayan word for demons roughly translates as "the great farters.")

There were several groups of people who were guaranteed to end up in the Upper World. Royalty and priests, already in communion with the gods, prepared for their deaths in such a way that their trip would likely have a positive outcome. Women who died in childbirth, warriors who died in battle, and people killed as human sacrifice were all guaranteed eternity in this heavenly place. It's not hard to imagine how it helped the rulers to promise joyful, eternal life to those who gave of themselves to help the kingdom by having children, going to war, and becoming sacrifices.

The kings themselves spent much of their lives preparing for their deaths. When a common person died, the person's family buried him or her under their hut, then moved out and built a new hut, using the original one as a shrine for their departed ancestor.

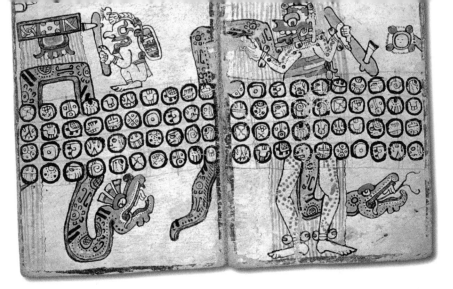

The Madrid Codex is a Mayan hieroglyphic manuscript that describes which god to worship on each day of the 260-day sacred calendar. This page shows the god of the dead fighting with the serpent rain god, Chac.

Kings took this practice to a whole new level. The tomb of the king was built inside the ultimate pyramid or "mountain" in the city. The Maya believed entrance to the Underworld was on a river that wound through a giant cave inside a mountain. Therefore, during their lifetimes, the Mayan kings employed many workers to build their own replicas of a mountain, inside which were secret tunnels and passageways that would begin the journey through Xibalba to the Upper World. The king's tomb would be hidden inside. Once a king died, the next king would begin construction of his own tomb on top of that of the king that went before. Thus the temples of the last king would become inner chambers of the next king's tomb, and the pyramid would rise in height. By the time several kings had been buried in a mountain, it could stretch up eight to twelve stories, towering over the lives of the common people below!

MAYAN CALENDARS AND THE UPCOMING END OF THE WORLD

In the Mayan world, priests and scientists were the same people. The early Mayan invented calendars the same way the Julian calendar (our current calendar) was invented: by studying the movement of the stars and planets. They soon realized there were patterns that repeated again and again, and that each group of stars traveled in its own path. In this way, they could predict when certain planets and stars would be near each other, and even when there would be an eclipse. Since the common people had no idea what an eclipse was, if the priest or king could make it seem like he had the power to make the sun or moon go dark, that was an awesome thing!

The Maya also held sacred a twenty-year cycle. It was at the end of the twenty-year cycle, called the "Katun," that they would finish and dedicate large buildings, go to war, or conduct any other milestone celebrations.

Perhaps the most famous of the Mayan calendars in current times is what they called their "Long Calendar." Mayan legend held that the world would be destroyed five times. The Maya believed the world had already been destroyed four times, and we were currently living in the last of the five ages of Earth. According to Mayan belief, the world was last reborn on August 13, 3114 B.C. This final cycle of days would last thirteen Bakuns. A Bakun is 1,872 days, which means the world is destroyed every 5,128 years.

Their calendar for this is called the "Long Count." According to the Mayan Long Count Calendar, the world will end for the final time on December 21, 2012.

Of course, some people argue that the world ended for the Maya 1,000 years ago.

WAR

Each city in the Mayan civilization had its own king, and its own government. Because of this, the city-states were almost constantly at war with each other. However, war didn't mean mustering large troops of men together to go fight each other. Instead, the king would consult with the priests to find a suitable day to attack. They'd choose the target city, and send out highly trained teams of scouts. It would be a secret raid. There would be no warning.

On the day of the war, the warriors from the attacking city would be in position. When the time came, they would rush into the city, with drums beating, loud shouting, and chanting, and make a run for the king, nobles, and warriors of the city. At this stage, the point was to capture them, not kill them—although they would kill anyone who attempted to fight them off.

If they were successful, they would march off with the losing warriors, priests, and king. This would decimate the power structure of the losing city, which would now owe allegiance to the winning city.

Once they returned home, the victorious king would hold a great celebration. The losing noblemen and king would be slathered with blue paint—the color of sacrifice.

Then the captured king would be brought to the top of the temple pyramid and killed as a sacrifice to the gods. (Mayans did not sacrifice their own people. That's why warfare and raids were constant.)

MAYAN BALL GAMES

A favorite pastime for the Maya were ball games. Each large city had its own courts, the largest of which was found in the ruins of the city of Chichen Itzá. Here a game was played with a solid rubber ball. A large stone ring was affixed to either end of the court, and players had to try to get the ball through using only their elbows, knees, sides, and buttocks. If you touched the ball with your hands or feet, you were disqualified. The outcome of these games was serious, because the captain of the losing team became the day's sacrifice to the gods.

THE FINAL MYSTERY

The Mayan civilization reached its highest point in about 800 B.C. From that point on, one by one, the greatest towns were simply abandoned. Over the next 200 years, each town abruptly stopped carving hieroglyphs and was deserted.

But why?

Through the centuries, different theories have been offered. Some archeologists believed the land simply couldn't sustain so many million people, and they slowly starved to death or wandered off in search of virgin land to cultivate. Others believed the end was aided by great natural disasters such as hurricanes and earthquakes or long-lasting drought.

Others believed that, as people began to starve, the sacrifices that the kings and priests made to the gods became more desperate, finally including men, women, and infants of their own tribes. The common people could have lost faith that their leaders were divine or able to help them, and began refusing to obey them.

In 2005, archeologists named Sylvia Alvarado and Tomás Barrientos made a chilling find in the abandoned Mayan city of Cancuén. Instead of finding carved obelisks detailing the great deeds of the final king, they found the final king, and his queen, murdered, and buried in a shallow grave. Only eighty feet away, in a cistern, or man-made pool, they found the bodies of thirty-one slain noblemen, women, and children. North of the palace, they found the bodies of another twelve nobles or priests. All of them had been murdered.

Some historians have guessed that the murders were committed by outsiders who subsequently marched off with the town's population, never to be seen again. Others take this as evidence that the common folk finally revolted, and killed the leaders who were ritually killing them to appease the gods—however, a lifetime of training left them respecting their leaders enough to take the time to bury them, and let them go to their graves in their finery.

What actually happened to these incredible city-states that each boasted their own man-made mountains and temples?

We still don't know. But new clues are turning up when they're least expected.

OPPOSITE PAGE: Two men examine an artifact of the ancient Mayan culture in Quirigua, Guatemala. (COURTESY OF THE LIBRARY OF CONGRESS)

3.

ATLANTIS

POSEIDON AND CLEITO

According to the ancient Greeks, Poseidon, a god and ruler of the ocean, fell in love with a beautiful human woman named Cleito. Poseidon won the heart of Cleito. Together they eventually had five sets of twin boys, who were each half god, half man. The oldest of the boys was named Atlas.

Poseidon was jealous of Cleito's beauty, so he found a lush island and built canals as moats, with rings of land inside them. In the very center, he built a palace for Cleito, where no other suitors could get to her. Poseidon named this country "Atlantis," after their oldest son.

The country thrived, ruled by the sons of Poseidon and Cleito. The people of Atlantis were prosperous and lived happy lives—until they became proud and greedy. When they tried to conquer the neighboring areas which would become the countries of Greece, Italy, and Egypt, the gods stepped in, and Atlantis was destroyed.

PLATO'S DREAM CITY

Stories about the lost continent of Atlantis persist to this day. The earliest written record of it comes from the philosopher Plato, who lived in Athens around 400 B.C. In his writings, Plato described Atlantis in great detail—as the most wonderful place anyone could imagine. It was a large, circular island with a huge stone wall built all the way around the edge of it. The outside, and by far the largest, ring of land was farmland so fertile it needed to be harvested twice a year. There was a canal dug in a circle that separated the farmlands from the next ring in. This canal had docks for sailing ships and for the powerful navy of Atlantis.

The next ring of land was surrounded by a copper wall. It was the leisure center of the city. In this location there were large parks, tree-lined boulevards leading to bath houses, gymnasiums for working out and playing games, stadiums for watching sporting events, race tracks, theaters, and horseback riding centers filled with horses. Plato explained that for the people of Atlantis, leisure time was not thought of as frivolous, but as the greatest good.

Past another canal was a smaller island ring, which was surrounded by a wall of tin. This is where the people of Atlantis lived, in shining, multistory homes filled with windows and light, and built around courtyards. At the corner of each boulevard was a fountain, where men and women sat to chat about philosophy and religion. They didn't need to draw water in heavy jars because they had hot and cold running water in their own homes. According to Plato, the colors of the city were brilliant. Of all the colors, the ones that stood out most were the red and black of the original stones dug from the Earth.

Many towers and terraces in this smaller ring had a commanding view of the final circle of land which was the heart of Atlantis. That was the citadel, the fortified center that could be protected against any attack. That inner island also held the schools and universities, as well as the palaces of the rulers, and temples to the gods.

The most magnificent building of all Atlantis was a temple to its founding god, Poseidon. The temple had spires reaching up to the heavens themselves. Inside was a giant statue of Poseidon on a chariot pulled by dolphins and sea nymphs.

Plato's writings describe the people of Atlantis as being intelligent and well educated. It was only when they became full of themselves and started attacking other countries that Poseidon became angry. He was so angry that he destroyed his beloved land of Atlantis. According to Plato, it was a "cataclysm"—a disaster so huge that Atlantis disappeared in a single day and night, never to be seen again.

DID ATLANTIS EVER REALLY EXIST?

Plato, who wrote the dialogues describing Atlantis, has been known as the father of modern thought and education. He told many parables and fables to make moral points.

But the story of Atlantis was different, he said. He said that the story of Atlantis was true.

Plato got the stories from the writings of Solon, a politician and writer from Athens who lived 100 years before Plato. Solon learned the stories during his travels in Egypt. Egyptian society developed writing early, and had libraries of books, mostly written in hieroglyphics, or picture writing.

So how much of the description of this beautiful city was Plato? How much was Solon? How much was Egyptian? How much was true?

THE MOST MAGNIFICENT
BUILDING OF ALL ATLANTIS
WAS A TEMPLE TO ITS
FOUNDING GOD, POSEIDON.
THE TEMPLE HAD SPIRES
REACHING UP TO THE
HEAVENS THEMSELVES.
INSIDE WAS A GIANT STATUE
OF POSEIDON ON A CHARIOT
PULLED BY DOLPHINS AND
SEA NYMPHS.

Many people have suggested that Plato's own opinions about what would make up the ideal layout of the perfect city—leisure pursuits, planned housing, beautiful temples, and universities—led him to embellish the descriptions of Atlantis that had been handed down.

Plato was also born a citizen of Athens, Greece. At that time, Athens was at war with the neighboring city-state of Sparta. This war went on for twenty-seven long years—from the time Plato was three years old until he was thirty. He felt the loss of men and resources was a bitter waste. At that time, Athens had a government called a democracy (a form of which the United States has today), in which leaders were elected. While Plato appreciated the idea of democracy, he felt that the leaders who made decisions to do things such as wage war often had a selfish agenda. In the story he told of Atlantis, he made it clear that the gods themselves are angered by such decisions, perhaps using the story as a warning and a scolding to the men who had caused Athens to be at war for so many years.

CLUES ABOUT THE REAL ATLANTIS

According to Solon, the Egyptians said that Atlantis had been destroyed 9,000 years earlier. He gave the location of Atlantis as beyond the Pillars of Hercules.

Even assuming that the story passed along to Plato was based on fact, there are several problems with deciphering it. For one thing, Solon claimed that Atlantis sank into the sea 9,000 years earlier. But 9,000 years earlier was still the ice age. It was prehistoric. No one had invented writing, so no one recorded any stories. Also, 9,000 years earlier, Egypt, Greece, and Italy didn't

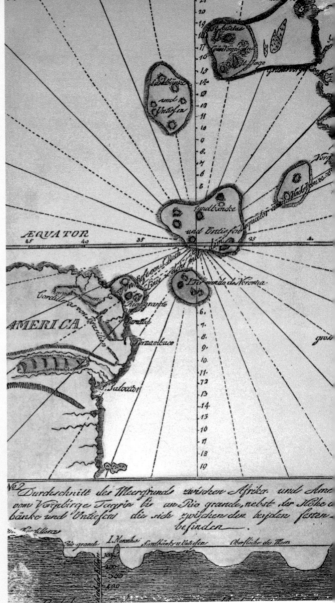

This 1785 German map shows pieces of Atlantis halfway between Africa and America—one of many guesses over the years! (© THE GRANGER COLLECTION, NEW YORK)

have cultures that were around to be invaded. There were no societies as Plato described.

Some scholars have questioned whether Solon, in reading Egyptian hieroglyphs, didn't misinterpret the characters and write "9000" when the symbols meant "900." Or, whether somewhere along the line, someone added another zero for emphasis: this happened a very, very long time ago—before our great-great grandparents, or anyone we know.

Dating the story of Atlantis 900 years before Plato starts to make sense. That would put the culture in the Bronze Age. This was the period in which humans had developed the ability not only to use big, heavy materials such as stone and iron but also to craft fine, delicate objects out of metals such as bronze. Humans were becoming master builders and master craftsmen.

The greatest challenge nowadays is to determine, from the information Plato gives us, where Atlantis was located. Plato says it is "beyond the Pillars of Hercules." No one today knows where the Pillars of Hercules were. Some have suggested the Straits of Gibraltar, where the Atlantic Ocean meets the Mediterranean Sea. Others have suggested the Pillars stood at an opening into the Aegean Sea. Hopeful explorers have looked for Atlantis in the Atlantic Ocean, and even as far away as in the Caribbean. The story does say that the navy of Atlantis attacked Greece and Italy, which would have been difficult from locations so far away.

AN ISLAND CALLED FEAR

What was the place that could have been the basis for the story of Atlantis? Through the centuries, explorers have sought to find clues to the location of that fabled place. Here are some of the main physical clues: It was an island society with a navy. Also, the stones from which buildings were built included naturally red, white, and black clay. It was known that bulls were worshipped. The society was very advanced to the point that they even had hot and cold running water indoors. And some terrible natural disaster happened that made the culture completely disappear, seemingly overnight.

Within the last century, many clues have pointed to the same place.

There once was an island in the Aegean Sea called Kalliste, which means "most beautiful" in Greek. The people of Kalliste had a fabulous lifestyle for the time. Their houses were among the most beautiful in the world. Many of them were three stories tall, designed with many levels and architectural flourishes. The walls were hand-painted with frescos, and their furniture was sumptuous and well designed. The people were educated and enjoyed art. Their kitchens were large and stocked with grains, meats, fish, and oils. The people of Kalliste had something else very rare for the time: indoor plumbing with hot and cold running water.

Some archeologists have said that civilization as a whole might have advanced much more quickly had Kalliste been allowed to flourish and to trade with other countries.

An artist's idea of what the island of Kalliste may have looked like during the explosive eruption. (© CORBIS)

So, what happened? In 1628 B.C., the volcano that had formed the island, and which sat at the very center of Kalliste, erupted. It didn't just explode, it sent fire and ash more than fifty miles up into the sky. It created earthquakes felt more than 2,000 miles away! And it created giant waves called "tsunamis" that would have wiped out coastal cities and naval fleets for hundreds of miles. Comparatively speaking, the eruption of Mount Vesuvius that destroyed Pompeii and Herculaneum was only a burp.

When the Kalliste volcano exploded, the earthquakes and tsunamis alone would have killed tens of thousands of people. And black soot would have blocked out the sun not only for days and weeks but also for months, possibly years.

Most spectacularly, the entire center of the island, which had been the cone of the volcano, sank completely. What remains above water today is a circular shell of what used to be an island culture.

The Greeks renamed the small sliver of island that remained. Its new name was Thera. It means "fear."

COULD THERA HAVE BEEN ATLANTIS?

No one will ever know for sure whether Atlantic actually existed. Certainly, the violent catastrophe that happened there would have been remembered with awe and terror by anyone who lived within hundreds of miles. It would also have been recorded in some form in nearby Egypt, Greece, and Italy.

There are other interesting clues. In the ruins that remain on the above-water parts of Thera, archeologists found many building stones of red, black, and white, as well as many frescos depicting bulls. They found evidence of indoor plumbing, with hot and cold running water. And the island of Kalliste itself was circular, as the main city of Atlantis was said to have been. Was the capital city of Kalliste laid out in circles? We won't know until the center of the island, which sank completely, is found undersea. The island is known today as Santorini, and the sunken center cauldron is a fantastic thing to see from the air.

FAMOUS SEARCHES FOR ATLANTIS

For thousands of years, people have hunted for the "lost continent" of Atlantis. Within the last century alone, it seemed there was a new urgency to find the country. Much interest was

aroused in the early 1900s when archeologists found astonishing ancient ruins on Santorini and the neighboring island of Crete that proved cultures existed that were much more ancient—and much more advanced—than anyone had supposed.

In the 1930s, the scientific branch of the Nazi government of Germany sent expeditions throughout the world looking for Atlantis. They believed the people who lived there had been the original Aryans, who were god-men. They looked for clues in places as far-flung as Tibet and South America.

Also in the first half of the 1900s, a self-proclaimed prophet named Edgar Cayce would go into trances and give messages he received. He reported that Atlantis was underwater in the Caribbean, and that it would resurface in the 1960s. Many of Cayce's followers headed for the Caribbean. They explored using scuba equipment, as well as more advanced technology to search underwater. In fact, to the surprise of many archeologists, they found several sunken cities. However, none of them had the sophistication of the legendary Atlantis.

When Plato told the story of Atlantis, did he report only what Solon had described, or did he embellish the story to echo his own values, and catch the imagination of his readers?

Where did Solon's original information about Atlantis come from?

These are questions to which we might never find answers. But the story of a perfect civilization, destroyed overnight, continues to excite each new generation.

ANCIENT CULTURE PLAYS TO THE CROWDS

Perhaps because of Edgar Cayce's visions and his reports that Atlantis was run by crystal power, Atlantis was embraced as a spiritual homeland by many participants of the New Age movement of the late 1900s, who claimed they were able to "channel," or speak with the voice of various people from Atlantis. The most famous of those is a woman named J. Z. Knight who lives in Washington State, and who claims to channel "Ramtha," a spiritual warrior of the Lemurian people. Ramtha himself claimed to have conquered the technologically advanced but spiritually bankrupt Atlanteans nearly 35,000 years ago (before the Ice Age!) when he was only fourteen.

According to Ramtha, Atlantis was in the Atlantic basin, under what is now the Atlantic Ocean. So far, no proof of this has been found.

Recent movies have also made good use of the legend. In *Journey to the Center of the Earth*, the adventurous characters come across the lost civilization. In Disney's animated *Atlantis: The Lost Empire*, the heroes find an underwater civilization run on crystal power.

4.

POMPEII

THE TIME MACHINE

Have you ever wished you could travel back in time? Not just to see a few relics from a certain place, but to understand who the people were, how they lived, what their everyday clothes looked like, what games the kids played, what they thought was funny, even what their graffiti said?

Probably the closest we'll ever come (until the invention of actual time travel) is to explore the ruins of the Italian city of Pompeii. For if you went back to visit 2,000 years ago, on a hot August day—the twenty-fourth of August, in the year 79, to be exact—in the morning, you'd find a bustling city of nearly 20,000 people. Servants were setting tables for lunch. Bakers had fragrant, round loaves of bread in the oven. Schools were in session, and the markets were open for business.

By 6:30 the next morning, everyone who remained was dead, and Pompeii was frozen in time under volcanic ash that would preserve the entire city exactly as it had been that day.

MOVE TO THE COUNTRY!

Roman history gives us information about Pompeii that sets the stage for its tragic end. By the year 79 A.D., the Romans had a very progressive civilization. Their capital city of Rome was unmatched anywhere in the world. It had amazing temples, theaters, coliseums, and imposing government buildings. The few wealthiest citizens lived in vast mansions called villas. However, the overwhelming majority of people lived stacked together in apartment buildings, much like in modern cities. Some wealthy Romans decided they could get nicer homes, even seaside villas, if they moved out of Rome. Many middle-class citizens followed their example, hoping for more space and a chance at the good life.

One of the cities of choice was Pompeii, a historic city down south, nestled not far from the Bay of Naples, under a beautiful mountain called Vesuvius. Pompeii was well situated for trade, with ports on both the bay and the river Sarno.

Because of its prime location, Pompeii had been a target for takeover by competing countries over the centuries. As a means of protection, the rulers of Pompeii eventually built a large wall all the way around the city to protect it from invasions. Eight gates provided entry to and exit from the city, two in the wall on each side.

DAILY LIFE

Life in Pompeii was colorful and exciting. The city itself was easy to get around in, whether on foot or horseback. The streets were laid out in a grid pattern, with the streets and sidewalks exactly as wide as the two-story homes were tall. Large homes were mixed in with smaller apartments, and businesses were built into the residential parts of the city, so that each block was a mix of bakeries, clothing stores, laundries, food shops, stores that dyed cloth different colors, anything that was needed for daily life. Sidewalks were raised a foot above street level, so people could walk without fear of being trampled by chariots or donkeys which passed in the streets below.

The sons of the wealthy went to school, and most of the daughters of upper-class families were tutored at home. Education was very highly valued.

One of the busiest parts of town was the Forum, the center of religion and government, where ideas were discussed and debated. There were many temples for worship, built to a wide array of gods, including Isis, Apollo, and Jupiter—who was the patron god of the town, and therefore got the best temple. The Forum also served as an open-air shopping mall, with two stories of shops running along either side.

The citizens of Pompeii valued good entertainment. They had a theater district, which included a large theater for spectacles and a small theater where local companies produced plays. There were restaurants that specialized in different kinds of food—including some of the world's earliest salad bars!

A large part of everyday life was going to the public baths—what we would call gyms or spas. There were many, and they were nicely designed with workout rooms, large pools with cool water, and smaller heated pools, as well as courtyards to hang out and talk with friends. Men and women went to separate baths. These were the daily social centers of the town.

By far the most exciting—and most controversial—entertainment in town took place at the coliseum, a huge outdoor arena. It was here that gladiators, who were slaves trained to be expert combatants, fought. In 79 A.D., the coliseum in Pompeii had only recently reopened. It had been closed by order of the Emperor after a particularly heated match had caused passions to run high among the spectators, and several people in the audience had been killed in the melee that followed.

GLADIATORS: THE ROCK STARS OF POMPEII

Armed combat to the death was a favorite sport among the people of Pompeii. They would buy tickets for matches between gladiators in their city's own coliseum, a huge open-air arena. Gladiators were slaves who were extensively trained in combat. Once a slave was purchased to be a gladiator, he was sent to the special training center in Pompeii. There he lived, slept, and ate combat. When he was finally judged to be ready, he would make his debut in the coliseum.

Throngs of people would come to watch the popular gladiators fight. There would be posters of them all over town, and graffiti artists would draw their likenesses and talk about their popularity with the women.

Fights were a betting sport. If a gladiator you bet on won his match, it was traditional to give him a "tip"—which often amounted to a lot of money. Good gladiators quickly became very wealthy.

The term for being a gladiator—assuming you didn't get killed—was three years. If you survived, you could buy your freedom with the money you'd earned, and often have enough to buy yourself a nice villa and become a business owner.

Sometimes a gladiator would kill his opponent, but more often a match would end in either a draw or surrender. Of course, the gladiators who found fame were usually the victors.

Criminals were executed at the coliseum during the lunch break, so you were certain to get some death for your ticket money. Sometimes they were killed by wild animals. Occasionally, criminals were forced to act out parts in dramas that told stories of the gods or great heroes. The catch was that if you played the part of someone who got killed in the story—you really *did* get killed. Sometimes the convicts had to fight for their lives, even though they were untrained. If they happened to be good at combat, it didn't matter. They had to keep fighting opponent after opponent until they died.

SLAVES

If you lived in ancient Pompeii, odds were that you either had slaves or were a slave. And, you would have had almost as good a chance of being one as having one. In fact, four out of every ten people who lived in Pompeii were slaves.

Slaves were not necessarily uneducated people. When there was a war, the soldiers on the losing side were captured as slaves. Some were undoubtedly foot soldiers, but others were officers who came from wealthy families back in their home country. In Pompeii, all the doctors, lawyers, teachers, builders, actors, and gladiators were slaves.

Romans allowed slaves to purchase their freedom by saving money they made outside their usual duties. Also, many slaves were like part of the family, and often good masters freed their slaves out of gratitude when their services were no longer needed. They then became known as "Freedmen" and could go on to establish their own businesses. In Pompeii, some of the most luxurious villas belonged to Freedmen who became successful and undoubtedly went on to have slaves of their own.

POMPEII'S WALLS SPORTED MORE THAN 3,000 GRAFFITI SAYINGS. IN FACT, PUBLICIZING YOUR BUSINESS OR VENTING YOUR ANGER...WAS SUCH BIG BUSINESS THAT POMPEII HAD PROFESSIONAL GRAFFITI ARTISTS.

ELECTIONS AND GRAFFITI

Another form of entertainment in Pompeii was public elections. Officials were only elected for one year, so campaigning was constant. Only the wealthy had a chance of being elected, because office holders were expected to spend their own cash to improve Pompeii. Fountains, roads, and theaters had all been built by ambitious politicians with their own money.

The most accepted form of campaigning was to have graffiti written on the walls of homes and businesses in support of your candidacy. Pompeii's walls sported more than 3,000 graffiti sayings. In fact, publicizing your business or venting your anger ("Sameous to Cornelius: Go hang yourself!") was such big business that Pompeii had professional graffiti artists.

Some graffiti phrases found on Pompeii's walls included:
- *Profit is happiness!*
- *The city block of the Arrii Pollii in the possession of Gnaeus Alleius Nigidius Maius is available to rent from July Ist. There are shops on the first floor, upper stories, high-class rooms and a house. A person interested in renting this property should contact Primus, the slave of Gnaeus Alleius Nigidius Maius.*
- *A small problem gets larger if you ignore it.*
- *Cruel Lalagus, why do you not love me?*
- *O walls, you have held up so much tedious graffiti that I am amazed that you have not already collapsed in ruin.*

However, much of the graffiti on the walls of Pompeii is so risqué that a Latin teacher in Vermont was suspended in 2006 for having her high school students translate it into English!

OMINOUS RUMBLINGS

Most of the buildings in Pompeii and the neighboring cities of Herculaneum and Naples were built from local stone. What the residents in 79 A.D. had no way of knowing was that the kind of stone they chose for building was actually hardened lava, left 2,000 years earlier by the last huge eruption of the volcano in the mountain Vesuvius, situated right behind them. Since records didn't go back 2,000 years, they had no inkling that Vesuvius could be catastrophically destructive—or that it blew its top every 2,000 years—and their number was about up.

Seventeen years before, in the year 62 A.D., southern Italy had been jolted by a strong earthquake. Pompeii was hit hard. Roofs caved in, columns toppled, and a major reservoir broke, flooding the streets. The Temple of Jupiter was nearly completely destroyed.

The Roman Emperor Nero sent state funds to help the people of Pompeii repair their city. They were proud of how quickly their city was rebuilt—much of it made even grander than it had been originally.

But no one had the geological knowledge to tie the huge earthquake to the large, beautiful Mount Vesuvius. They never suspected that beneath the surface, the sleeping volcano was slowly waking up. In fact, up until that time, the Romans didn't even have a word that meant "volcano."

For seventeen years, between the earthquake of 62 and the twenty-fourth of August, 79 A.D., the people of Pompeii lived on borrowed time.

DOOMSDAY

Toward the end of August in 79 A.D., the people of Pompeii were a little on edge. There had been some rumblings under the Earth. Some streams had mysteriously dried up, and some wells suddenly had no water. Domestic animals, including dogs, cats, and horses, seemed nervous. There were sometimes choppy waves in the harbor, even though there was no wind blowing. These occurrences made for some interesting discussions in the marketplace, but no one knew what to make of it.

The morning of August twenty-fourth was a typical summer day—until lunchtime. Some households were just sitting down to eat. Some families were done with lunch and about to rest. Others were out in the marketplace, buying, selling, baking bread, or doing wash at the laundry. Then, without warning, it happened—Mount Vesuvius erupted.

Any volcanic eruption is dramatic, but what happened to Vesuvius that day has been seen by very few people who lived to tell about it. Fire, gases, and molten earth spewed twelve miles straight up into the air. Earthquakes started and kept on coming.

What should the people do? How long would the eruption last? Should they go indoors and wait for the eruption to be over? Or should they run? If so, what would happen to their homes and their things? Would they all be looted before they returned? And where should they run to? Who knew which town was safer than theirs? What if they made it to another town and got killed there, while Pompeii was relatively unharmed?

Looking back, it's easy to wonder why the people of Pompeii didn't just make a run for it. One way that can help us understand is by looking at how people responded when Vesuvius erupted in 1944. During that eruption, a whole river of lava poured down the side of the mountain and nearly wiped out a city to the west of it called Ottaviano. Most of the residents of Ottaviano were able to flee before the lava reached them. Two days later they went back and began to rebuild. People in the other towns stayed put and they were fine. Even now, when the dangers of volcanoes are understood, it's human nature for people to stay put and hope the volcano ruins the next village, not their own.

In fact, when Vesuvius started to erupt in 79 A.D., a famous soldier, historian, and naturalist, Pliny the Elder, got so excited about witnessing this event that he got in a ship and sailed from the safety of his home toward the volcano, staying with friends in a village on the shore around the bay from the eruption. Pliny the Elder took many notes. He thought it was a great adventure. But he, too, had underestimated Mount Vesuvius. He had asthma, and by the time the air was filled with gases the next day, he suffocated to death. Fortunately for us, many of the most vivid descriptions of the eruptions came from letters written by his nephew, Pliny the Younger, who was staying with him at the time.

Back in Pompeii, after the initial eruption, it took a while for gravity to catch up with the red-hot stones that had been thrown twelve miles into the air—but it did, and slowly they started to fall to Earth. They began hitting Pompeii and the surrounding cities and countryside like hail.

Many citizens gathered their families and ran for the gates of the city. Some of them stopped to pack up their most precious belongings. Some, as was discovered later, buried their jewelry and other precious items to keep them safe for their return. Others just dropped everything and left, with the tables still set for lunch and the dog tied out in the yard. Of course, most of them chose to run toward the south and east, away from the volcano.

They couldn't know it, but this was a bad choice for several reasons. One reason was because not everyone with their carts and horses—or even just thousands of people on foot—could fit through the eastern and southern gates all at one time. However, all of the 2,000 people who died in Pompeii were found inside homes or businesses—not dead from being trampled in the road. The first, less drastic, stages of the volcano lasted long enough that those people who chose to leave somehow managed to get through the gates.

But getting through the gates did not ensure that the residents would live. No one knew that within the next eleven hours, the area would be blanketed by poisonous gases from the mountain, and everyone in that area would die. The wind dictated that the gases from the volcano would blow south and east, the exact same direction that most people were trying to escape.

Direct accounts from the time indicate that a fortunate few people escaped the volcano's impact. Survivors either picked a lucky direction or they somehow traveled farther and faster than their fellow townspeople and escaped the poisonous, deadly gases.

Some people from Pompeii made it to the sea, many to docks of their neighboring town of Herculaneum. If they had access to a boat and left quickly, they probably survived. However, according to accounts of Pliny the Younger and others, within several hours the wind changed and the sea itself became full of ash and pumice. No more boats could sail.

Down by the docks in Herculaneum, hundreds of people crowded for shelter in boathouses under the docks. Here they would be found centuries later.

Over 2,000 people chose to stay in Pompeii. Even though the sky became completely black as the ash blocked out the sun, some people who were sheltered indoors likely survived until 6:30 a.m. the next morning. During that time, volcanic lava stone and ash started piling up like snow on streets and roofs. It fell at an estimated rate of six inches an hour, so after six hours there would have been about three feet of volcanic debris on most houses. This was enough to crash through many roofs. By the next morning, there would have been five feet of debris—so much that people could no longer open their doors to get outside.

By midnight of that first day, the eruption itself seemed about over. However, that's when the column of debris that had been shooting up collapsed. When it did so, all the hot stones, lava, and superhot gases started pouring like a huge river down the side of the volcano. During the night and the next morning, the column of ash collapsed five more times. It was the fourth and largest "collapse" that spelled the final disaster. But how would a mere collapse have completely buried cities the size of Pompeii and Herculaneum?

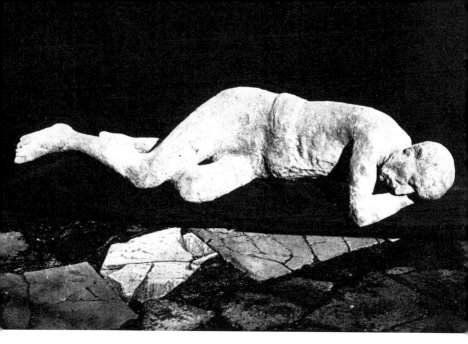

This cast was created from the imprint left by a man who perished in the volcanic event that buried Pompeii. (© BETTMAN/CORBIS)

A KILLER OF AN ANSWER

For 1,900 years, scientists could only guess at the magnitude of what happened at Pompeii. Then on May 18, 1980, Mount Saint Helens in the U.S. state of Washington had a similar eruption. And, like Pompeii, it wasn't any old volcanic eruption. The entire top (cone) of the mountain completely blew off. No one who studied volcanoes had seen anything like it in his or her lifetime.

Mount Saint Helens was not located above bustling cities, but even so, fifty-seven people, 7,000 animals, and millions of fish and birds were killed by the explosion. The ash cloud grew to 80,000 feet within fifteen minutes.

BY MIDNIGHT OF THAT FIRST DAY, THE ERUPTION ITSELF SEEMED ABOUT OVER. HOWEVER, THAT'S WHEN THE COLUMN OF DEBRIS THAT HAD BEEN SHOOTING UP COLLAPSED. WHEN IT DID SO, ALL THE HOT STONES, LAVA, AND SUPERHOT GASES STARTED POURING LIKE A HUGE RIVER DOWN THE SIDE OF THE VOLCANO.

When the cone blew, the largest landslide in recorded history swept down the mountain at speeds of 70 to 150 miles per hour and buried much of the Toutle River under an average of 150 feet of debris. Some areas were covered by as much as 600 feet. Not only that, the sideways, or "Lateral Blast," roared out of the north side of the mountain at 300 miles per hour. That means within minutes it created a 230-square-mile fan-shaped area of devastation reaching a distance of 17 miles from the crater. With temperatures as high as 660 degrees Fahrenheit and the power of twenty-four megatons of thermal energy, it snapped 100-year-old trees like toothpicks.

The ash from the eruption of Mount Saint Helens on the West Coast of the United States reached the East Coast (3,000 miles away) within three days. Fifteen days later, ash had circled the whole Earth.

The scientists now understood what happened during that fourth eruption of Mount Vesuvius.

For, according to the records of Pliny the Younger, at 6:30 in the morning following the eruption, the cone exploded and roared through the cities below like a hurricane of wind, fire, and lava, devouring everything in its path. It ripped off roofs and blew in walls and windows. The poisonous gases from deep inside the Earth came with it. Anyone still alive suffocated to death.

In the months that followed, some survivors came back, trying to find their belongings and loved ones. But the town was so deeply buried it was hard to dig down to. Also, there were still many pockets of poisonous gases trapped inside the town, making it dangerous to dig. Finally the survivors gave up and continued their lives in other places.

THE LEGEND

For hundreds of years, the legend of the town of Pompeii, and its neighbor Herculaneum, were kept alive. But after so many years, the story sounded more like a myth than the story of real cities.

Pompeii remained buried, and forgotten, for 1,500 years.

The closest anyone came to rediscovering the city was in 1594, when an architect was digging an underground channel to bring water from the Sarno River to a rich man's villa. The workmen came across bits and pieces of old buildings, and even found an inscription that said "decurio Pompeiis," but they didn't realize what they'd found.

In 1709, some workmen dug through to the ancient theater of Herculaneum. However, the prince who owned the land wasn't excited about the historic find. He only wanted precious treasures for himself. So he had the workmen loot the theater, but then they stopped. The volcanic material was too hard to dig through.

Finally, in the 1860s, an archeologist named Fiorelli arrived. He was aware of the historical importance of the city, and began digging carefully. Fiorelli instituted strict guidelines about how the dig should take place. He divided the city into blocks and roads. Every object they found was properly recorded and catalogued. Finally, the reemergence of Pompeii had begun.

Thus they found the entire city just as it had been at noon on August 24, 79 A.D. Bakers had bread in the ovens, tables were set for lunch, mosaics were on the walls and floors, and graffiti was painted all over town.

Of course the bodies of the people had disintegrated over the years. However, the exact shape of how they had been when they died, the clothes and shoes they wore, and even their expressions of horror or pain or peacefulness were preserved in the lava. Fiorelli discovered that if they poured plaster into the hollow shapes in the lava where the bodies had been caught—and had finally disintegrated—they could make sculptures of people just as they had been.

By doing this, they found fathers sheltering children, dogs on leashes, donkeys grinding wheat, a man cradling a woman as they waited together to die; the family of a pregnant woman as they waited with her.

EVEN TODAY

One hundred and fifty years after the excavations began, the whole city of Pompeii has not yet been unearthed. Painstaking work is still going on. However, there is also a debate between factions of archeologists. Some say no more of the city should be uncovered, for once the ancient buildings are exposed to the air, they begin to break down by the natural wear and tear of the elements. It is a difficult choice to make, when unearthing the ancient city will eventually mean its destruction.

But in the meantime, Pompeii again has come to life—frozen forever on that August day.

And above the Bay of Naples, Vesuvius stands, once again hitting the 2,000-year mark since its last cataclysmic eruption. Yet people live and work and go about their daily lives in Naples and the other nearby cities.

Will history repeat itself?

Only time will tell.

5.

In 1860, Henri Mahout walked into the Cambodian jungle look-ing for plant species that were unknown in his native France. What he found instead was a fabulous city that had never been seen by Westerners. Even the Cambodians only spoke of it as a legend—a lost city, "hidden by the gods," full of beautiful tem-ples and treasures beyond imagination.

A botanist by training, Mahout had begun a journey through Asia in 1859. When he arrived in Cambodia, a French mission-ary told him that the peasants spoke of "temples built by gods or giants" now in ruins deep in the jungle. Intrigued, Mahout hired local guides and set out to see for himself.

In the previous fifty years, two British explorers had set out to find the fabled city, but they reported finding only scattered remnants of ancient buildings. We don't know whether Mahout was simply luckier than they were, or his guides better, but he succeeded where the others failed. Here is how he described it:

Ruins of such grandeur, remains of structures that must have been raised at such an immense cost of labor, that, at the first view, one is filled with profound admiration…. One of these temples—a rival to that of Solomon, and erected by some ancient Michelangelo—might take an honorable place beside our most beautiful buildings. It is grander than

anything left to us by Greece and Rome, and presents a sad contrast to
the state of barbarism in which the nation is now plunged.
—HENRI MAHOUT'S DIARY

The city and its magnificent temple seemed to him too grand to have been built by the ancestors of the peasants who populated Cambodia in the nineteenth century. He assumed that it was evidence of a great people who had mysteriously vanished. But he was wrong. Historians now know that this fabulous city was once the capital of a great civilization in what is now Cambodia: the Khmer Empire.

Mahout spent the next three weeks drawing sketches of the temple. It is now called Angkor Wat, which simply means "city temple." To this day we do not know what its builders called it. We do know that it is still the single largest religious building in the world. With a circumference of almost four miles, Angkor Wat is larger than the great cathedrals of Europe, the Vatican, the temples of the East, or any of the pyramids. And it is only one of a thousand temples in the city of Angkor!

A year after making his discovery, Mahout died of fever in the jungle at the age of thirty-five. His servant carried his diaries to Bangkok. They were published in France in 1863, drawing the world's attention to this little-known corner of Southeast Asia. Other explorers and scientists visited soon after. So did the curious. Probably the most famous visitor was Anna Leonowens, the British-born governess in the court of the king of Siam. Her life story would later be the basis of Rodgers and Hammerstein's classic musical, *The King and I*. She visited by elephant in the

1870s, after reading Mahout's diaries. Fortune hunters came, as well, carting off artifacts to Europe. Most importantly, historians and archeologists began the work of examining the site and trying to understand the history and purpose of the ancient city with its temples, government buildings, and waterways. That task continues to this day.

The great temple of Angkor Wat, in present-day Cambodia, is the largest religious building in the world. (© JOSON / ZEFA / CORBIS)

THE CITY OF ANGKOR WAS... CONSTRUCTED OF SANDSTONE BLOCKS TRANSPORTED MANY MILES BY OX CART AND MOVED AROUND ON THE SITE BY ELEPHANTS. THE PROJECT TOOK THIRTY-SEVEN YEARS. THE QUALITY OF THE ENGINEERING THROUGHOUT THE SITE IS PHENOMENAL.

WHO BUILT ANGKOR WAT?

One must ask, what has become of this powerful race, so civilized and enlightened to create these gigantic works? Oh, sad fragility of human beings!

——HENRI MAHOUT'S DIARY

Fortunately for the archeologists who arrived hoping to coax the ancient city to give up its secrets, the temple's walls were covered with inscriptions. It turned out that those inscriptions were written both in Sanskrit and in an ancient form of Cambodian that is similar to what is spoken today. Therefore, both languages were fairly easy to translate. The stories on the walls revealed that the builders of Angkor Wat were the ancestors of the contemporary Cambodians.

One thousand years ago, Angkor was the capital of the vast Khmer Empire, which ruled much of Southeast Asia. It included large portions of present-day Thailand, Cambodia, Laos, and Vietnam. The city became prosperous because it was located in a perfect spot on the trade route between India and China. Archeological and historical evidence suggests that around a million people lived in Angkor in its heyday.

Historians tell us that the city of Angkor was founded in the ninth century and abandoned in the fifteenth. King Suryavarman II began building the grand Angkor Wat in the first half of the twelfth century, at the peak of the empire's wealth, power, and influence. It was constructed of sandstone blocks transported many miles by ox cart and moved around on the site by elephants. The project took thirty-seven years. The quality of the engineering throughout the site is phenomenal. One example is a six foot by six-hundred-and-sixty foot corridor with measurements accurate to within a fraction of an inch.

WHY WAS THE GREAT TEMPLE BUILT?

Most archeologists believe that Suryavarman II built Angkor Wat as a "funerary monument"—a giant tomb (like the pyramids of Egypt) built for the burial of a powerful ruler. They base this theory on the fact that the temple faces west, unlike the other buildings in the city. In ancient Hindu cultures, funerary monuments always faced west.

The great temple is shaped like a pyramid built in three tiers, surrounded by a giant moat filled with water. Visitors report a strange experience when they cross the raised road leading over the moat to the temple. The water reflects the sky above, and they feel as if they are suspended in space. That effect is probably exactly what the builders intended. Modern archeologists believe that the temple was designed to represent the Hindu conception of the universe. At the center of the temple are five towers that symbolize the peaks of the mythical Mount Meru, the home of the gods and the center of the universe. The walls and other structures stand for layers of mountains, and the moat represents the sacred ocean, the source of life.

The temple is dedicated to the Hindu high god Vishnu. Its walls are filled with "bas-reliefs"—carvings in the stone—depicting stories from Hindu mythology. One of the most famous of these carvings is called "The Churning of the Sea of Milk." In it, Vishnu supervises as gods and demons churn the sea

of life to produce the elixir of immortality. Another bas-relief depicts the battles of the gods, while yet another narrates the accomplishments of the Khmer rulers—particularly the temple's builder, Suryavarman II.

HOW DID A JUNGLE CITY SUPPORT ITS POPULATION?

Besides telling stories about the gods and rulers, the temple walls also depict the ancient residents of Angkor. They reveal that then, as now, life centered on fishing and growing rice, the staple of the Khmer, and today the Cambodian diet. Providing for more than a million residents, and feeding the armies that kept order in the vast Khmer Empire, required several plentiful rice crops every year. How did the ancients manage this feat?

Some modern scientists believe that the ancient Khmer built a sophisticated water management system to irrigate the massive rice fields. It is certainly true that the city of Angkor is full of waterways—dikes with walls thirty feet high and forty feet wide. At full volume, this system has the capacity to hold forty-nine billion gallons of water. French scientists spent years developing and testing the theory that these reservoirs were constructed by the Khmer to capture the water during the monsoon season, when the rain was heavy. Then they let the water out during the dry season to irrigate the rice fields.

But a British archeologist named Elizabeth Moore has a very different theory. She studied the city using high-altitude radar. This technology can be used virtually to see into the past by discovering tiny traces of structures that existed hundreds of years before. Moore did not find any evidence of irrigation canals. She also studied the many wall inscriptions depicting daily life. She found that none of the inscriptions has anything to do with irrigation. That seems odd, if irrigation was so important to the Khmer.

Why, then, did they build all the waterways? Elizabeth Moore thinks they were built for religious reasons: like the temples, the waterways were a tribute to the gods. Interestingly enough, it appears that the grateful gods did provide for their faithful people. At certain times of the year, water that normally flowed away from the city turned around and flowed toward it!

Here's the scientific explanation: huge amounts of water fell during the monsoon season. The water swelled the great lake called the Tonle Sap. Then the water of the Tonle Sap, which normally flowed away from Angkor toward the Mekong River, backed up and overflowed toward the city. This created vast flood plains, which watered the rice crops and also caused fish to spawn in huge numbers. The people had food in abundance.

WHY WAS ANGKOR WAT DESERTED?

Historians have various theories to explain why such a great civilization collapsed. Some suggest that a famine might have weakened the people. Others say that the trade routes may have shifted, taking away the Khmer's economic base. Some even speculate that the Khmer's obsession with building ever more gigantic and elaborate water systems so distracted them that enemies were able to swoop in and conquer the city.

Whatever the reason, in about 1431, the Khmer were defeated and enslaved by invaders from Thailand. They had been fighting with that neighboring country for many years. In the years before final battle, the Thai capital had been moved to a site perilously close to that city. This bold action may suggest that the Thai people were gaining the upper hand. Typically, victorious invaders carried off a conquered people to serve as slaves. That may have been the fate of the remaining Khmer.

But though the city was abandoned, the temple of Angkor Wat continued to be used, in far humbler fashion. Even though the temple was built in honor of Hindu gods, by the time of Angkor's fall it had become primarily Buddhist—the other great religion that originated in India. One way we know this fact is from the diary of a member of a Chinese diplomatic party who spent a year in Angkor in the thirteenth century. It was translated in 1902 as *Memoirs on the Customs of Cambodia*. The author calls the people "barbarians," noting that the king had five wives. He also says, "Worship of the Buddha is universal."

For four hundred and twenty-nine years between 1431 and 1860, Buddhist monks took refuge in the temple. They, along with the wide moat, probably kept it from being as ravaged by the encroaching jungle as the other buildings in Angkor were. When Westerners arrived they found many Buddhist statues that had been left over the centuries. Most of these have been removed in an effort to restore the temple to its original luster, but today Angkor Wat is an active Buddhist temple.

Though Angkor Wat was built to honor the Hindu deities, it has been occupied by Buddhist monks for centuries.

(©ANDREW/HOLBROOKE/CORBIS)

THE SECRET CODE OF ANGKOR WAT

Art historian Dr. Eleanor Mannikka probed the mysteries of Angkor Wat in the 1990s. She measured the temple's structures in detail. The unit of measure she used was the same one employed by the Khmer builders—a hat, which equals the distance from a person's elbow to the tip of the middle finger.

What she discovered astounded her. The measurements formed a kind of code. They recorded with incredible accuracy the cycles of the sun and the moon, significant dates in the history of the Khmer rulers, and even dates relating to the Hindu "time of the gods" (which is to say, their mythology).

She also found that the architects designed the temple to make use of the path of the sun through the sky. Their calculations were so accurate that on important religious days, the sun's rays would illuminate symbolically important carvings. One example is the way that, on the spring equinox (the first day of spring), a bas-relief of the king and the god Vishnu in the great tower would be framed in a natural spotlight. This "light show" symbolized the Khmer belief that their earthly rulers were divine.

Dr. Mannikka believes that the temple's design served an even deeper purpose. In Hindu mythology, the world moves through four eras, or ages. Each age is called a yuga. The Khmer priests understood their world to be in the Kali Yuga, the worst of the four. It would last 432,000 years, so no one living could hope to see the end of it. But a person who moved through the temple to its center would travel symbolically into a better age. They would experience being in the presence of the gods. She believes that the temple was constructed to protect the people from the negative forces of the Kali Yuga.

Was Angkor Wat built to save the world? Dr. Mannikka's theories have been both praised and disputed. It is hoped that future research will bring us closer to the truth.

WILL ANGKOR WAT'S SECRETS EVER BE REVEALED?

For many years during the twentieth century, it became impossible to study Angkor because of the war in nearby Vietnam. The situation was made even worse by the reign of terror of Cambodia's former ruling political party, the Khmer Rouge regime. Its leader, Pol Pot, committed mass murder against his own people, killing an estimated 1.7 million or more. Even after the fall of the regime and the death of Pol Pot, the area around Angkor remained strewn with land mines.

Today the visitors to Angkor Wat are back, both researchers and tourists. Many of the questions still remaining about Angkor will one day be resolved by science. Excavation under the Earth, which is typically how archeologists get most of their information about life in ancient cultures, has only just begun.

But the deepest mystery of Angkor will likely never be explained. It's the question raised by all of the towering wonders built by human hands from ancient times to today. What is it that drives the human race to construct monuments of such superhuman magnitude? Is it human ego, religious awe, national pride? Or is it something beyond all of them? That's a question we cannot answer, but only stand in awe and wonder.

CHAPTER NOTES

The following section offers the sources of the quoted material found throughout the book. The first and last words of the quotation are followed by its source. For full citations on each source, please see the Sources section on page 82.
The following source abbreviations are used:

NG (National Geographic)—*Splendors of the Past*
Kallen—*The Mayans*

Opening Quote
Page
vi   "One must ask…beings!" NG, p. 86

Chapter Two: The Maya
Page
20   "I am entering…ground!" Kallen, p. 17

Chapter Five: Angkor Wat
Page
67   "hidden…gods," NG, p. 86
67   "temples…giants" NG, p. 86
76   "Worship…universal." NG, p. 86
78   "time…gods" NG, p. 86

SOURCES

BOOKS

Andrews, Ian. *Pompeii*. New York: Cambridge University Press, 1978.

Atkinson, Austen. *Lost Civilizations: Rediscovering Ancient Sites Through New Technology*. New York: Watson-Guptill Publications, 2002.

Caselli, Giovanni. *In Search of Pompeii: Uncovering a Buried Roman City*. New York: P. Bedrick Books, 1999.

Collins, Andrew. *Gateway to Atlantis: The Search for the Source of a Lost Civilization*. New York: Caroll & Graf, 2000.

Connolly, Peter. *Pompeii*. Oxford: Oxford University Press, 1990.

Gruber, Beth. *National Geographic Investigates Ancient Iraq: Archaeology Unlocks the Secrets of Iraq's Past*. Washington, DC: National Geographic, 2007.

Kallen, Stuart A. *The Mayans*. San Diego, CA: Lucent Books, 2001.

Moorey, P.R.S. *Ur 'of the Chaldees': A Revised and Updated Edition of Sir Leonard Woolley's Excavations at Ur*. Ithaca, NY: Cornell University Press, 1982.

National Geographic Society. *Splendors of the Past: Lost Cities of the Ancient World*. Washington, DC: National Geographic Society, 1981.

Spence, Lewis. *The History of Atlantis*. New York: Bell Publishing Co., 1968.

Stevens, John L. *Incidents of Travel in Central America, Chiapas, and Yucatan, Vol. 1*. Mineola, NY: Dover Publications, 1969.

Vanags, Patricia. *The Glory That Was Pompeii*. New York: Mayflower Books, 1979.

WEBSITES

UR:

Story of the Royal Tombs of Ur:

  http://www.mesopotamia.co.uk/tombs/story/sto_set.html

  http://www.globalheritagefund.org/where/ur.html

Private homes in Ur:

  http://s8int.com/phile/page45.html

  http://www.mnsu.edu/emuseum/archaeology/sites/middle_east/
  ur html

MAYA:

  http://mayaruins.com/

  http://www.civilization.ca/civil/maya/mmc01eng.html

  http://encarta.msn.com/encyclopedia_761576077/
  maya_civilization html

POMPEII:

Pompeii Graffiti (edited):

  http://college.hmco.com/history/west/perry/western_civilization/
  6e/students/primary/pompeii.htm

In Mouhot's Footsteps: http://ronemmons.com/biographies/mouhot/

DOCUMENTARIES

Atlantis [video recording]: *Mystery of the Minoans* / CineNova Productions for
  The Discovery Channel; produced by Jane Armstrong, Nancy Burton;
  directed by Christopher Rowley, Jane Armstrong; written by Gary Lang.

Cities of the Underworld: Maya Underworld. Lost Civilizations. Produced by
  Time-Life. Executive Producer, Joel Westbrook. Series Producer, Jason
  Williams. 500 minutes total. Narrated by Sam Waterston.

Pompeii: Buried Alive. Produced by Multimedia Entertainment, Inc. and
  Filmroos, Inc. in association with A&E Network.

INDEX

Note: **Bold** page numbers indicate photographs and captions.